EXCESS
BAGGAGE

POEMS & OTHER WRITINGS

by
Ken Gum

Published by Ken Gum, Traverse City, Michigan

Design: Brandon Hoffman, Village Press, Inc.
Editor: Jason Smith, Village Press, Inc.

ISBN: 978-0-9815812-1-7

Printed in the United States of America by Village Press, Inc., Traverse City, Michigan

For Dad and Tom

Introductions by the "Floccinaucinihilipilificators"

Author's note: Floccinaucinihilipilification *is the longest (non-scientific) word in the* English language. According to the O.E.D. it means: "the action or habit of estimating as worthless." This is not particularly relevant other than as an example of what our little coterie of friends talks about at our Thursday evening meetings. After debating the fact that this was indeed the longest word, we dubbed our group "The Floccis."

Since its inception on St. Patrick's Day 2004, The Floccis have continued our weekly tradition of meeting at a local establishment for wine, good food, and engaging conversation. Consisting of a trial attorney, a retired orthopedic surgeon, a wildlife artist, a well-known author, an ophthalmologist, and occasionally a lawyer/scrap metal recycling company executive, our group brings many different thought processes to the table. Our common thread of yearning for knowledge and wisdom, our love of language and literature, and especially our respect for a good joke has kept us together. We have shared many spiritual experiences in the natural world as well as each of our inner worlds... things that many would not expect a grown man to do.

Ken Gum
Traverse City, Michigan
2008

• • • • •

Ken Gum, in this wonderfully personal anthology, is a man of science examining the human soul through the microscope lens of verse and essay. He's a romantic with a sense of darkness, and a storyteller with a light sense of irony. The voice of the outdoorsman, which he was born to be, trades quips with the voice of the surgeon, which he became. Both are profound, critical, astute observers.

If you walk in the woods or the water, you'll probably walk a little differently after reading Ken's work. He turns over a lot of stones as he hunts and fishes his way. He muses, "These stones were placed by God," then he straightens up, looks you in the eye, and tells you the truth he makes of what he's seen—the sacred and profane, the trivial and the exalted, the mud and the rain.

Enjoy this vivid writing and this vivid point of view, or, I should say, points of view. There are two very different people—the outdoorsman and the surgeon—telling us about the world around and inside.

Grant Parsons, Esq.
Traverse City, Michigan
2008

H erein lies the soul and distillation of life's questions, pain, and joy... insight into relationships... the dissolution and reawakening of desire... universal truths to men of passion and conscience.

Yet the gift of Ken's voice is most lucid when he speaks of nature's wonders.

This is when I know him best.

Wordlessly, we have worshiped together at the altar of the Creator. Green drake duns and seven-pound brook trout on Labrador's Minipi; whip-poor-wills, beaver, deer, and wise, old brown trout on *Hexagenia*-blessed AuSable River evenings; rainbows sipping PMD's; Rock Creek, Montana; cutthroat pushing a bow wave toward a damselfly on the mirror surface of Georgetown Lake, with you, still as a heron, line coiled in the lupine at your feet.

But more than the catching, we have enjoyed the bond of true friendship. Sitting together beneath virgin white pines on the bank of a pristine Michigan stream, sharing so much, with and without words. Silverpink bonefish tails flashing in the first rays of sunrise... shoulder to shoulder... *double!*

Back at the lodge, the enveloping peace of a Bahamian summer evening. Cribbage and bourbon... exchanging verses of poetry... reciting favorite lines from Tom Robbins.

We have shared life's greatest riches.

Thanks Ken, for opening your heart and life to us. With remarkable range and depth you have put into words what most of us, in our mutual search for truth, cannot.

As Rilke said, "Be patient toward all that is unsolved in your heart and try to love the questions themselves like locked rooms and like books that are written in a very foreign tongue. Do not now seek the answers, which cannot be given you because you would not be able to live them. And the point is, to live everything. Live the questions now. Perhaps you will then gradually, without noticing it, live along some distant day into the answer...!"

David Lint, M.D.
Traverse City, Michigan
2008

• • • • •

I have thought, prayed, and worried a little about what I would write for
my part in this introduction to Ken's thoughtful collection of poetry. How
does one sum up in a paragraph or two what a friend he'd do anything
for means to him, especially with my limited vocabulary (a shortcoming he
never fails to remind me about)?

Simply put, there's so much that makes up Ken that it's tough to know
where to begin—his devotion to a wonderful family; the thriving practice he's
created with his God-given talent for medicine; his faith and wisdom; his
constant tweaking of my grammar; his hilarious victory dance on the rare
occasion when he bests me at cribbage; his companionship in the grouse
woods and duck blind; a mutual love of bird dogs; his wealth of information
on trout (and various, less desirable species) and how to catch them; his
love of conversation; his perverted sense of humor and seemingly benign,
soft-spoken way of getting his point across while still poking fun at me; his
willingness to do good by anyone he meets.

From our October bird hunts to sipping wine on a streambank while
waiting for the hatch, to watching our kids play together, to in-depth discus-
sions about life and death and everything in between. Where to begin indeed.

When it comes right down to it, what I love most about him is that he's
one of those rare, unconditional friends we always hope to find but seldom
do, and one we strive to be more like but seldom are. That's Ken—a true
friend. It's a favor I'm not sure I can very adequately return, but I'll always
try. As long as I keep beating him at cribbage and shooting more woodcock
with fewer shells, that is.

Christopher Smith
Interlochen, Michigan
2008

● ● ● ● ●

The living forest is in a constant cycle of death and rebirth. Ancient trees that once bore witness to the many passing seasons regrettably must die, as all life. Without their passing however, sunlight could not shine through to the forest floor to stimulate and nourish new growth. To read the poetry of Dr. Gum is to travel the same cycle of death and rebirth; to feel the pain of death and regret, and the resulting joy and hope of new growth. Savor the journey....

Ronald Gostek, Esq.
Chicago, Illinois
2008

●　●　●　●　●

ACKNOWLEDGEMENTS

Thanks mom for encouraging me to pursue this project. You have been my rock from the beginning. A special hug to my wife Marilyn and children Zane and Zoe who were the inspiration for many of these poems.

Many years ago, I made the mistake of reading too much. After realizing I could never satisfy my thirst for the knowledge I desired, I slowed down and took a systematic approach. A few Bibles, the Greek philosophers, and eventually through classic literature and on to thinkers like Kant, Thoreau, and many others. After my psyche had become overwhelmed by this, I sought out virtuous writers like Tom Wolfe and Jim Harrison. Tom Robbins has always given me a special little tingle. My point is that everyone who has written a unique sentence has a special place in my heart. They push me on. They have made me a better person for having read their work.

I would also like to thank the Floccis. You have made me feel not so alone in the world. My friends, colleagues, and co-workers in the field of medicine make the thrill of caring for people feel like the privilege which it should be. And a special thank-you to Donna Rodgers, my friend, secretary, medical technician, and all-around good person who did most of the work in putting this collection of writings together. And finally, thank-you Steve and Jason Smith at Village Press for your generous contributions, encouragement, and expert editing. And to Chris Smith, my very talented artistic friend who provided the cover sketch and illustrations (drawings).

Ken Gum
Traverse City, Michigan
2008

PREFACE

This collection of poems and other drivel is dedicated to Plato and blamed on Emmanuel Kant. It is for my friends...past, present and future, many of whom have a collection of their own writings far superior to this. Jim Harrison once wrote, "It never ceases to amaze me what a complicated set of emotional baggage your average human being carries around with them." These poems emanated directly from my soul with very little intellectual re-engineering (as you will soon see for yourself) and are an invitation into the deeper levels of my search for truths. It has occurred to me that all too seldom, we allow our friends a glimpse into the inner workings of our mind, perhaps for fear of embarrassment, or lack of acceptance.

The information we seek is perennially available to us in bookstores and libraries everywhere, yet we typically and complacently choose to learn only what is readily available and provided to us in a format dictated by the media. Decide for yourself what you are interested in learning and seek it out, not passively, but actively. The answers to your questions are out there but the chances are quite good that you will not find them until you put down the remote control. As Thoreau stated, "Surely another may also think for me, but it is not therefore desirable that he should do so to the exclusion of my thinking for myself."

WHO AM I

Once again I sit in the trough,
caught in the emotional maelstrom of ontological limbo.
I believe there is an air pocket
of meager confidence
several leagues down.
I listen carefully for a *bluup*
to reach conscious levels.
I practice omphaloskepsis
but I am an omphaloskeptic.

•   •   •   •   •

GONE

Sing the song of Rubicon
our childhood will soon be gone
a dreamless sleep with nothing left to ponder.

What is wrong with wine and song?
Feed the weak, starve the strong?
But who will feel the dreadful burning hunger?

Elapsed the time of hocus pocus,
forced in turn to focus
on the shackles and the whip with sweated brow.

Gone are dreams and hopes and lotus
burned the letters which He wrote us
our hands yet frozen to the fetid plow.

THE PUZZLE

And can it be that all I am
is pieces of life that
are in the past?

Or am I here and now
existing, thinking of all the
things that will not last?

As I figure out the forms
and colors of the puzzle
it finally comes together.

Realizing that today, yes today,
begats tomorrow and
tomorrow is forever.

. . . . .

WHAT IS LIFE... REALLY?

I explain myself in algorithms (even to myself),
maintaining a dignity that only few can share.
Content with mere existence,
then exulting in it.
These stones were placed by God.
Not man.
And the fly engulfed realizes his re-enactment.
The play has netted trillions of dollars
and no one has spent a dime.

THE ACT

Blue acted out his lines nightly,
casting his light on all those around him
while the footlights
shone brightly in his face.

Yet he carried on at his particular wavelength
caring not to mingle his color with their whiteness.
He had been separated by the prism
and they were unaffected.

"I am not short," he replied to Red
trying not to be like Green;
but as you may have noticed by now
Blue was quite yellow.

The footlights dimmed to test him
and Blue began fading to gray.
Frightened, he accidentally ran into Black
and never came back.

THOUGHTS OF DEATH

There is an odd will
within me that can't wait
to die.

No suicidal wish or
vogue gallery of the maudlin,
just pure, grim curiosity.

I drink life like it is
a '64 Margaux and find it
pleasurable but hollow.

A gift.
A glimpse.
A teaser if you will.

But to me,
death, which we dread, may be
the birth of understanding.

Dread locks.
Hope opens.

I know that the large door
leads to real life.

LANGUISH

The air of discontent,
must not become cement.
I must remain intent,
on things of great portent.
Sing and not lament,
provide and not prevent,
and not misrepresent,
those truths held eminent.

The single implement,
the greatest testament,
the final element,
is faith incipient.
My dreams incognizant,
the words put into print,
aren't insignificant,
they've purpose and intent.

Desire is not for rent,
it's ours and permanent.
Remain intransigent,
but most of all content.

• • • • •

WHY

There is a question
that has been haunting me lately,
especially on these warm autumn days
when we walk through the beautiful woods
wanting to see everything:
Why do gnats have an affinity
for our eyes?

DUPLICITY

The common ground cannot be found
between the fields and fallow.
The hot and cold can grow old
between the deep and shallow.

We look for worn-out clothes to wear
and try to be most common.
But the things we cherish most in life
are the things we lay our trust on.

• • • • •

SUPPORTED

We sat as friends
accepting, waiting for large mayflies.
Bobbing, supported on wings as if
suspended in porcelain.
Sipping, tasting life's pleasures together
and then dying into reality
or the mouth of a trout.

A NIGHTMARE

The horror, the horror,
the nabobs, the jungle
intercede in the mists
of algae and fungal
growths extending from
decaying nostrils and ears
from imaginary scenes
in which I appear
to fall unsupported
into uncharted waters
without friends, without foes,
without mother or father,
alone at last
the darkness of space
into myself not leaving a trace
of the realness
which I have become
it never begins
it never is done.

THOUGHTS WHILE LEAVING THE WOODS

Friends, I ask, may we freely forecast our fate?
Being of the patrician hordes, allowed access to the best minds,
I can tell you
we may not.
So carry the carcass of the noble beast proudly
on spent shoulders
and don't look back, for the hunt was a good one.
The gut pile
of reflection already calls the flies to the feast.
Well developed organs,
once a tiny cluster of cells,
lie warm,
steaming against the dying ferns of Autumn.
Passages newly created,
allowed access to heart and lung,
leaking life from within.
Hastily the spirit vanishes,
we pray,
carried away on the sanguine mist.
Golden leaves falling
recalling the magnificence of this once whole creature.
A circle
opened by a larger force, allowed and sustained by the same.
Silence surrounds as eyes gloss.
The game filled with life and motion
gives way to paranoid stillness.
Stunned,
the world slowly resumes its pace, interrupted,
as if starting in too high a gear,
not reaching speed until the inimical intruder
withers from its ranks.
Intangible and complex.

The subtle series of events bring the two together
for the plan goes infinitely backward and forward
conception to death.
Life repeated generation upon generation
each with its unique influence and influences
have resulted
in this chance meeting.
Knowledge of all past and present,
prerequisite to prediction is never possible, only imagined.
Each plays an inherent role incognizant
of how and why.
Ask questions at the risk of suffering
ontological ignorance.
Once realized we do not stop,
but go on.

THE PHYSICIAN

I, to the betterment of mind or body, cannot decide
which best to devote time,
for the minutes rush away, line screaming from the reel
uncontrolled,
the strike coming too fast for senses to react or comprehend.
Washed in and out of thought
like plankton in the surf
I wait patiently for the tide to go out,
then wade into the silt at my own pace
picking, choosing, searching, finding
on hands and knees in the filth
whatever minutia I have yearned for
in more turbulent seas.
Call me healer,
yet being racked and torn,
split,
divided from youth
and carried by the mudslide to valleys unwanted,
how might I deserve such a title?
Soothe my disturbed body and aching mind,
all energy having been spent,
I cannot proceed further up the correct path (much the more difficult)
but stumble with the lost hordes into this world
and not the next.
Agonizing exertion, supremacy always penultimate to the result
this is what pushes, coerces, prods and connives me.
I bear this in addition to the despair of the others.
Thousands, millions in a lifetime come for answers
realizing the implicit fruitlessness of their questions.
You are blind
comes the reply.

Thus perceived, the anger builds,
neither can help each other at first.
And then there is one,
just as the ocean begins to swell and I slip under,
no mind and very little body,
senses removed one by one,
intolerable torture to observe,
faces turn away in pity or disgust,
yet this one is the raft to which I cling.
No particular wisdom or prowess, this isolated one
calls to me and saves me.
This one allows me to see in the midst of the tide,
what I had yearned for beneath.

ON PREJUDICE

I wish I were a black man
so I could appreciate all this change.
Puerile society, slap and torture it.
Make it understand.
We sing so loudly yet it only reverberates
in our skull.
Who hears but the black man?
Who can see the darkness but him?
We, with our sinecures and sophisms
attempt to deceive
only ourselves.
Recede into your bowers and sip mint juleps.
It is eleven o'clock and all is well.
Moral parsimony, it kills me.
A good roll in the muck is what we need,
yes,
go build a pyramid,
but don't tell me what clean is
until I've seen you dirty!
My god, how short and beautiful life is,
tell me how you waste it on hatred and petulance,
while the black man awaits the denouement,
the cotillion of good nature, human nature,
benevolence.
We should all wish we were black men.

LET'S GET A GRIP

And just where does it come from anyway,
this idea that we are in control,
while our children kill each other in the streets,
and we sentence ourselves to death by lethal injection
or hanging.
While disaffected minorities struggle for equality as human beings,
and lives are lived at the whim of a television commercial,
an evangelist,
or rock star, a designer, an actor, a teacher, preacher, poet or philosopher.
And physicians deliver the *coup de grace* to those who cannot
possibly endure the pain that is part of life.
And the need for money blinds us to the needs
of our fellows, and the lack of it
causes us to throw ourselves from penthouse balconies
to further litter our filthy sidewalks below.
When our technology, which has evolved to make our lives better
has not tamed mother nature but ruined her
and stultified our own ingenuity.
While our schools drift further from the wisdom of the ancients
and the lessons of history toward the barren shores of hard science
and simple syllogistic thought.
And our eminent democratic form of government
continues to breed mediocrity
not only in our leaders but the masses as well,
while the truly great ones seek solitude for their own protection
knowing they would not be understood or accepted.
And we continue in our ignorance to elect
ignorant, unqualified, uneducated, and undisciplined leaders
because we hold the hope in our hearts, even in soundest sleep,
that we too have the right to rule, should we be motivated to do so.

When the connection to our past has been buried so deeply
beneath the mantle of conformity
that each successive generation becomes more solitary,
alone and lost within itself,
unaware that its strife is not novel
but an immanent, recurrent phenomenon of life.
Where does this idea come from anyway?

ROY'S SQUIRREL

A fat boy in a sleeveless black
Metallica T-shirt shuffles along the
mid-western road early Sunday
morning as Roy approaches the squirrel
on his way to church.
He witnesses the head bowed
not in deference
but in despair.
Slumped shoulders signify the end
of a long, weary, hopeless night.

The squirrel bats the acorn
across the road two bends down the hill
as Roy, proceeding slowly, contemplates
recent mistakes.

The fat boy sees the squirrel first
throws a fistful of gravel as it
scampers away,
returning to joust
just moments later.
The fat boy shuffles on hating everything.
Roy had started to like himself
again
just as the tire
struck the squirrel.

GOD'S FUNERAL

I was alone at God's funeral
and wept,
tears pouring from my soul.
I searched desperately
for another to share my misery
but found no one.
Just silence and an empty room.
Where were all the others?
So many had been invited.
Were they frightened,
afraid to participate
in such an auspicious occasion?
The social event of a lifetime
and yet I stood alone.
Perhaps they had misread the invitation,
or had gotten lost
on the long, branching, treacherous road
winding its way along the mountainside
to the small mortuary
at the top.
I stepped outside briefly
listened carefully for the sound of voices
and was overcome by the resplendence
of the sun-drenched valley below,
the sweet whisper of the fresh air
through the leaves overhead,
the pleasant odor of the pines and
at once felt not so alone.
Rejuvenated,
I returned to the darkness of the tiny funeral parlor,
and to my amazement
the casket was empty.
God was gone.
Or had He ever been there?

SCULPTING

He was born, and fell at once into skillful loving hands,
moulding with special mixtures of exotic clay and sands.
With the finest tools available, they added and took away;
he was soft and thin, and change came easy, a little every day.

The fine manipulation was enjoyed right from the start
with the greatest expectation, that life could mimic art.
Their satisfaction grew as time went by for they had the perfect plan,
with a lot of loving labour they'd have the perfect little man.

As his form took shape, with pride and glee, they'd show him to a friend;
why the very nature of their selfless task, the means must justify the end.
Then at last one day they both stepped back and looked at their creation,
they knew beyond the shadow of doubt he'd create a great sensation.

They embraced and took a restful sigh, their work had been completed,
and with thoughtful recollection, nothing at all had been deleted.
They clung to him for quite a while, the flag remained unfurled
until their perfect little figure forced his way into the world.

With a slight amount of sorrow, they watched him leave the page
still content that through their sculpting he would safely come of age.
The clay had finally hardened and his form was firmly set;
they knew that all the work they'd done, he wouldn't soon forget.

But the weather in the world back then was harsh out on the range,
with all the rain and wind and ice his form began to change.
The sharpness of his perfect features became a little rounded,
and when his creators saw him they seemed to be dumbfounded.

How could this be, they asked themselves, we used the finest clays,
we baked him in the finest oven for days and days and days.
They rushed him to their studio and inspected all the damage,
then they ordered up some harder tools to fix what they could manage.

At first they tapped and filed and were gentle as could be,
but they knew that drastic measures were the last necessity.
The largest gilded hammer struck its blow, and with a start;
they fell to knees and wept, for he cracked and fell apart.

WITHOUT LOVE

Often we follow, in hot pursuit of perfection,
and become hollow, losing our direction.
Starting to rise above, startled to find,
we are alone... without love.

Wishing and waiting, answers elude us;
fighting and hating, emotions influence
actions, then push comes to shove
and we're alone, without love.

A clock will strike twelve, again on a whim,
lined up on the shelf, there are so many of them.
The fall from the pedestal can be very rough
when we're alone again... without love.

Sigh long and hard, the end appears near;
we let down our guard, a woman appears.
Apparition or real? Instinctual rebuff,
and at last we rejoice, we've learned to live without love.

• • • • •

A SECRET LOVE
(My personal favorite)

How this spring of love reflects
the glory of an April day,
which now shows all the beauty of the sun,
but a cloud takes all away.

And sanctified hearts made earnest in their union
as the clasping hands in prayer,
send silent signals hence unrecorded,
which only they can share.

YOU

I feel as if a sweater torn,
which no one cares to mend,
yet all will go on wearing me
until the bitter end.

And off to love of distant past
this awful yearning sent,
not knowing that the seasons changed
or what these feelings meant.

I wish that I could clone myself.
I've tried to no avail.
The lonely days, the sleepless nights
have left a bloody trail.

But on we go with heart in hand;
the world on which we fell
is not so kind, and only you
can break this binding spell.

THE TEMPTRESS

The woman with smiling crescent eyes sits
across from me and asks,
Why do you continue to mask sorrow with anger?

Because I wait. I do not enjoy the waiting,
nevertheless I wait.

You do not wear this bitterness well, she says.
When will the waiting end?
Perhaps now, perhaps never,
perhaps I will be sad and angry for so long that it will lose meaning.

I could make you happy now, she says.

No

I am not done with the waiting,
I am not ready to be happy quite yet.

How will you know when it is time, she asks.

I do not know, but if I wait long enough
the answer is sure to come.

Does the waiting cause you anger?

No

The anger allows me to wait, it gives me peace.
Please go now, allow me to enjoy my sorrow.

MY TALK WITH GOD

I went down to the river today
and spoke with God.
His answers were clear
though spoken in the language of the whip-poor-will.

We started out quite simply.
Would the trout rise tonight?
The answer, a plaintive... no.
No matter never mind, I said
tempting the reductionists, I just wanted to talk anyway.

The discussion escalated,
why do I feel so small today?
Because you are,
yet you could be quite large, came the answer.

The nighthawk burbled from above,
follow me, learn how to fly to happiness.
But I have no wings and certainly no feathers,
I'm only human.

The otter said close your eyes, use your soul
you can be anything you wish to be.
Look at me, am I not happy all the time?
I fly, too, but under water.

God, how did I drift away from you?
Look at the river, the raccoon chortled,
it flows, does it not, and all life drifts freely in its currents,
and the currents eventually take you to the ocean.
That is where it all ends, in the ocean.

A single trout then rose and spoke,
you are free to swim;
you can choose which ocean you end up in.
Simply choose, the consequences are the result of your choice.

You're afraid to choose aren't you, hooted the owl.
Afraid to choose.
That is why you have not started swimming.
Listen to the trout, use the currents to your advantage.

The firefly flashed its code,
look for the light inside.
You've had it shaded for so long,
let it shine through and it will direct you.

The bear sat next to me, don't be afraid.
Protect yourself, swim to shore and think,
then jump into the river and swim,
for your life.

THOUGHTS ON MIDLIFE

Approaching midlife, it has recently occurred to me that having spent myself on lowlifes and scoundrels, i.e. that Whitmanesque approach, my time has been dismally wasted. He must have had a much stronger ego than my own, hoping to bestow upon those less blessed, his virtues and wisdom, in the hope that "spreading the wealth" might lead to his own Nirvana. Now I am weary of the associations with others whose emotional and intellectual depth neighbors that of the Great Salt Lake and is commensurately just as lifeless.

I envision a single tree, roots deep into the rocks in a mountainside, withstanding the onslaught of an avalanche. Greed and superficiality pushing on all its branches until it is finally pulled from its moorings and dragged downhill, falling into a heep of debris with rescue unlikely as no one knows of the disaster. I dream of a mountainside covered with trees, standing close by each other as the deluge comes. A few may fall but they, with their strength, slow and eventually stop the torrent. The next year their offspring take root farther uphill until the risk of the avalanche becomes inconsequential.

So is the way of people and political systems as compared to nature. Just study it and realize that over the eons, the supremacy of any natural system has preceded the course of our brief human existence and systems. For now, I'm willing to stand firmly at the side of the mountain and watch as gravity exerts its effect.

THE PRISON

He came home from work kicking shoes off
and hugged her from behind
then collapsed on the couch grabbing his favorite book.
Dismissing the greeting, she continued about her trivial labors
then left with the dogs.

They climbed into bed gazing at Jay Leno
like two fey fast food cooks
until the freedom of sleep overtook them
and they dreamed pleasant dreams.

I have to get going, he said
as the alarm clock was punched off.
Do you want coffee this morning?
No thanks, I'm late.

The next night he returns home
from work very late.
Why didn't you call?
I'm sorry, I ran into so-and-so,
Goodnite.

The morning sun illuminated her sleeping face.
She's beautiful like this, he thought
slipping out of bed not wishing to interrupt
the serenity and happiness.

They sat across from each other at dinner that night
hoping for the distraction of a phone call
or a friend stopping by.
Their dialogue did not penetrate the surface of things.

The vacation started well,
the newness refreshing, it allowed distraction from the sorrow.
As they sat across from each other at the seaside café
open air allowed the gentle breeze to keep his cigarette smoke
away from her.

She conversed in German with another tourist,
smiling like a child.
She's beautiful like this, he thought as he ordered his fourth beer.
Would you like another, he asks
hoping to eventually speak to her in her own language,
no matter what it was.

Let's go, I want to be alone with you, she replies.
Bring me a shot as well he beckons to the waiter.
The breeze had died and he blew his smoke consciously away,
I wish you'd quit, she admonished.
The next drag he blew towards her and they left.

I want to do this today, she says when they awaken.
Whatever.
He took her there, they left.
It'll be nice to get back home,
Yes, he agreed.

He watched her sleeping on the plane.
She's beautiful like this, he thought
as he brushed the hair from her face
knowing that soon they would be home
and it wouldn't be so nice.

THE SECOND HALF

Flashes of yellow from aspens
trigger fond memories of a timely vacation
last summer
with the one I was supposed to love.

Hunting companions unaware
as we pass familiar sites where smiles occurred,
or a kiss took place
or where I netted her trout as she grinned from ear to ear.

The history hurts,
or rather the gaping crevasse between
the then and the now
that I have fallen into.

One may claim that all those years
of togetherness aren't lost;
they can still be fond memories.
Bullshit.

There has to be continuity
in everything.
All must come full circle for fulfillment.
It is gone.

Panick-stricken, feeling lost in the woods on a cloudy day,
there is no correct way to turn;
but if you don't know where you're going
any road will take you there... I guess.

Grandmother says keep your head held high,
don't lose your faith.
God I love her, and you.
Never forget that.

Time for round two, the bell has rung,
so put up your dukes, I'm coming out of my corner swinging.
The second half of the play,
after intermission, is always the best.

THE PERMANENT VISIT

She entered my life through the back door.
I knew she would be arriving soon,
I could smell her.
It was a sweet smell, with a hint of lemon.

She smiled as she snuck in quietly,
making sure the screen door didn't slam behind her.
The wind was from the South
and it was a sunny evening; warm but not too hot.

Her presence was not a temporary thing;
she had to stay and we both knew it.
This was not just a visit,
she had brought all her belongings, including her dog.

Her touch made me smile,
and gave me that warm satiated feeling
like a good glass of wine
following a very large meal.

She loved me, and all my stuff.
I gave her what little I had
and she graciously accepted.
I could tell by the light in her eyes she was happy.

The weather turned gloomy one evening
but I didn't really notice.
The lamps all seemed to burn brighter
with her around.

We sat before fires enjoying their sensuousness,
the warmth, the flickering flames, the odor of the burning aspen.
Later, we unpacked her things and put them into drawers and closets,
turned out the lights and went to bed.

SUBSTITUTION
(For Marilyn)

They left and waved good-bye to me,
the ones I thought I knew;
they said the thought of her replacement
was more than they could do.

I tried to explain the loneliness
I felt inside my soul,
that all the friends in my small world
could never fill the hole.

They watched from the distant hillsides
as the transition was taking place,
they gossipped, chided, scorned, and quipped
and spat into my face.

As time went by my heart grew stronger
her love was at my side;
the loss of any, all my friends
did not affect my pride.

All my life I'd watched them
as they clung to me and learned,
the lessons I had taught them all
that real friendship is returned.

Now I sit alone and wonder
why the lessons have all ended,
just when I could teach them how
real love can't be suspended.

It carries on regardless
of what others think this time.
The void is finally filled
by this newfound love of mine.

She gives me all I need and more,
the rest you can infer;
and leave us now, we'll be just fine
because all I need is her.

A NEW SOUND

She heard a new sound today,
which touched her deeply.
I could detect the disguised joy in her heart
though she never really told me.

It was a real sound
that echoed in the valley of life,
and brought a new vitality to us
as we trembled.

Amazing that such a subtle thing
could stir the human heart
to the point of tears,
which have only just begun.

The sound came from both of us
yet it seemed so foreign.
But somehow we both knew we would be able
to understand this new language.

As time went by we became aware
that the sound was growing louder.
It would soon enter the room
and become the life of the party.

The sound that initially frightened us,
even though we created it
slowly blended into the most beautiful harmony
that we will listen to every day for the rest of our lives.

MY BOY LOVES ME
(for Zane)

He says, "Hey dad can you do this?"
as he curls his tongue and
whistles for the first time.

He crosses his legs in the
easy chair and munches on chips
just like I do.

He watches an emotionally charged
movie with intensity of thought
well beyond his years.

He counts to twenty and grins
ear to ear when I say I'm
proud of him.

He takes things in stride
like when we were late to pick
him up at the bus stop from school.
He knows I love him.
It doesn't matter.

He wants to go fishing with me.
He loves it when we do things
alone together without mommy
or his sister.

I think he's proud of me, too.
He remembers everything, and
his honesty borne of innocence
reveals his only true thoughts
and feelings.
Even if he couldn't speak, I
would know.

He loves to sit next to me on
the couch with my arm around him.
He is strong but sensitive.
He cherishes my praise and
encouragement.

He knows that when he is
disciplined that love is still
in store and appreciates the lesson.
He trusts me.

He misses me when I'm away.
He hugs me when I come home.
He is courteous and kind.
He is creative and smart.
He reminds me to buckle my seatbelt.
He is left handed.
He is a bad dancer like me.

He is my best friend in a
very spiritual way.
His favorite color is orange
like the sun in the morning.
He likes it that he is taller
than the ferns now and can
walk with me through the woods.
He can entertain himself for
hours with the simplest of things.
He occasionally climbs into bed
and falls asleep with his head
on my shoulder and doesn't say
a word.

He wants to be a fisherman when
he grows up.
He already knows what life is all
about, the things that I
have forgotten.

A SMALL GIRL

(for Zoe)

Breathes life into me
as the sun peeks into my bedroom
and the paddling footsteps
echo in the hall.

Get in here and give your dad a kiss!
"Good morning, I love you."

Becoming a person is such
a beautiful thing.
"Eskimo" "Butterfly" mingle with truth
as kisses exchange love.

Demure readings belie
personality.

And then the nightly yawn
between "forgive us our trespasses" and
"forgive those who trespass against us"
allows me to sleep.

FREEZING TIME

If there has ever been a moment
at which I wished time could freeze
it is now.
Four blue eyes look into mine
attempting to draw inspiration from me
or inflating my pride with god-like authority.
Sweet innocence compelling me to
drift back in my own life.
Everything so new for them
so old for me.
It is so... nice to see the world
through young eyes again, thank you.
Dreams of success pale now
where they used to engulf me.
Anger and stress drift away more quickly
as I recall the Eskimo kiss goodnight.
Hatred and fear, emotions once common,
seldom surface as my thoughts constantly return to
"Daddy, I love you."
I have now felt love for the first time
and my parents' admonitions were true.
If they could just stop changing now,
right now.
If I could freeze this moment forever
just to have time to absorb it completely.
If only I could keep them from growing up
and being like me.

LET LOVE RULE

The storm forlorn, conceived and born
then swallowed by the beast.
Intransigent, he stayed and went,
and missed the mighty feast.

At night the flight with little light
perched on the limb of love,
Hell bent he went for want of rent,
but circled high above.

One day she came, no shame no blame
and helped him build his nest.
He pulled away and tried to play
as she held him to her breast.

The thoughts they shared, so scared, impaired
cut straight through to the soul.
Their bond created, so underrated
was way beyond control.

At last the past, the cast, the fast
was cut off in a flash.
Now all beware and all take care
these two create a splash.

The wave, close shave, now just behave
they taught their little one:
Let love rule and don't be cruel
until it all is done.

ON FEELING ALONE

Piercing sorrow envelopes the soul
as alienated friends, uncertain with their loyalties
await the next move.
So difficult to understand and absorb,
you pity them,
and then yourself.
You have spurned one who loved you with all her heart
and now you miss that love;
you have chosen to give yours to another.
The complexity of emotions is nearly too much to bear,
one minute relief, then fear.
Happiness bounces off the wall
returning to you as guilt and sorrow.
You call out to your new soulmate for reassurance
and she gladly provides it
and you throw the ball back against the wall.
Knowing that your actions are consistent with your will
you regain an odd form of integrity,
the lies slowly grinding to a halt.
You walk away before the ball bounces back again.

The comfort and familiarity once known are gone;
you find yourself awash in the surf
knowing you will eventually end up on the beautiful sunny beach,
but no one is there to witness your plight
or help you if you swallow some water.
No one will kill the fatted calf for you now,
you have fallen from the pedestal,
lost respect for yourself, and yearn for the old ways.
You would give anything for that peace of mind
that comes with consistency.
She reminds you that change can render consistency again.

A vision of that free and gentle love,
effortless, giving, unconditional
keeps you moving on your course.
The backward glances become less frequent.
The pain gives way to hope.

TO BE FOUR

I have become crippled,
not so much from age and physical ailments,
but from what I know.
I felt much better about things
when I was four.
When I was four
I would awaken my parents
at 3:00 in the morning to see if
Santa had come.
I could smell the rain coming.
I observed, undistracted by grief,
and only worried about the toad
I found being swallowed by a garter snake.
I told my dad that he should go talk
to my mom.
And I told my mom that dad wanted
to talk to her
when I knew they were angry with
each other and not speaking.
My plan worked.
When I was four my dad woke me up
at midnight to watch *The Time Machine*.
I felt so proud and loved.
When I was four everything was new
and exciting.
A T.V. dinner was fun.
I wanted to be a grown-up very badly
so I could do things with my dad.
I wanted to be tall enough
to ride a roller-coaster.
I finished everything on my plate.
Waste not, want not.

I watched the assassination of JFK on T.V.
I had no idea what wars were about.
Or hatred.
Or prejudice.
Our phone number had five numerals (9-8316)
that were dialed, not punched.
And when the phone rang I answered it,
Gum's residence, Kenny speaking.
When I was four I started kindergarten
and was nearly killed by a car passing
my school bus as I got off of it
on the very first day.
It was a black car, I fell to the road
and it went right over me.
I remember my mother screaming.
Now I am screaming,
I want to be four again.

WAITING

The days swing by like a pendulum
as you wait for the gravity of the situation
to bring everything to a halt,
and the earth's rotation to start everything
moving in the opposite direction.

You're watching a tennis match
with an endless volley;
the players outstanding
but no one scores.

Time does not bend from your perspective
because you are standing still,
yet that star you are watching
is not exactly where it appears to be.

For the first time in your life
you realize you're not in control,
but your helplessness is of your own making
and you wait.

LET IT GO

Happiness well within life's reach,
he touches but cannot grasp;
paralyzed as if in a nightmare,
falling.

His capacity for action hindered by moral shackles of his own making
while he watches others easily pass him by
smiling.

Fearing honesty that it might destroy the false world
that took years to create;
afraid of the emotional pain, which he knows he will have to endure
and the guilt built into the foundation
crumbling.

Knowing that his needs and desires may be too great
for anyone to endure,
he cannot even live up to his own expectations of himself, yet
laughing
he carries on, anesthetizing himself with mundane pleasures.

The deeper meaning pushed into the shadows, not ready yet,
too much living to do,
leave him alone, forgive him for he knows not what he does,
to himself.
Angst.

The self or the others, he meditates, who should I live for?
He subtracts nothing from the praise due to benevolence
but only yearns for justice
for all those whose lives and acts are a blessing to mankind.
Ah, herein lies the rub: his desire for happiness depends upon
the act of making others happy.
Reduced,

to his 28 cents worth of minerals and water he attempts to start
from scratch.
Emerging from the womb gasping for air, his first breath creates
a cough, it is toxic.
He yearns for the shelter of creation, wanting to be simply
the mixed genetic milieu of two single cells
joined into one; conception, life, reduced to its simplest terms.

But as life continues, the cells divide, and he re-creates himself
accidentally a clone and a clown, disguised as a human being.
And finally, understanding the fruitless nature of his pursuit,
he strips his costume and allows himself to be content
being the clown.

RANDOM WEEKEND THOUGHTS

There is something inexplicable about losing a friend, mentor, or parent. All of those times when you are "pretty sure" about words or actions, but are not quite ready to act them out, you may seek the advice and support of these people or at least know that they will be there to back you up. When they are gone, you may recollect their advice but still feel as if you are diving into the deep end of the pool without knowing how to swim, pretty much every day for quite a while.

When it comes to medicine, my career, this sort of mentor is appreciated but not absolutely necessary, as I have textbooks and journals to back up my decisions. However, when it comes to life, and the choices we have to make, the loss of a mentor can leave you feeling so alone and insecure that any unusual random event playing against your favor may reduce you to a heap of blubbering idiocy.

As I try to climb the ladder of wisdom and confidence, I cling with kid gloves to the slippery steps of my history with my mentors. Thus far they have allowed a firm grasp. But with each step skyward, I feel their influence and support become more distant and less secure. I pray that the gloved hand doesn't slip and require me to start from ground level again.

"As if written to Tom, back in the old email days of New Zealand"

Much has been written about rivers as a
metaphor of life, here's my shtick, they flow. Sometimes
quickly, and sometimes eddy. They change
in character slowly over eons, and suddenly
with the deluge. Yet they continue to flow.
They rise, they fall. Sometimes vibrant and
sometimes melodical, sometimes turbulent
and sometimes totally silent.

I want to encourage my children to take
the time to sit quietly by a river for several
hours on a regular basis. Watch passively,
listen closely, smell the redolence, dip your
fingers into the water just to feel the
temperature. Then taste it and wipe the
water on your jeans.

Tonight a hummingbird actually sat on my
shoulder for a moment. I'll remember that
moment when I eventually drift away on life's
own current. An otter swam by at that
deliquescent dusk time when people are
inside doing what people do and the river
life truly comes alive.

The river can teach. The river lives. The
river cares not about debt, anger, depression,
jealousy, social status, or its importance
in history. It just continues on doing
what it was intended to do. People have

contrived notions of how important people
are. The river is not contrived except
that it must laugh at us occasionally.
I would, if I were a river. The river
knows who created it. People don't.
So... to my children: Pay attention
to the river. It has much to teach.
You will learn much more in your life
from listening to the river than you
possibly could from any university,
parent, book, or art form. The river
will always be there for you. You should
always be there for it and with it. God is in the
river.

• • • • •

SILENCE

While vocalization is one man's virtue,
silence may be another's.
This silence may be solemn
as a cold, windless night in the North,
or horrifying,
as is the deafening silence of the multitudes.
One can lose himself totally
without thought or care,
but upon entering that truly silent realm
we slowly come back
and the realization of ourselves
can in time
prove the most priceless gifts.

THE END OF AN ERA

The knight is closing in,
his lance of bravery, honesty, courtesy
pierces my heart and the old one dies.

Yes, a picture is worth a thousand words
but a poem is worth a thousand pictures
yet we choose not to read.

Alone, we sit;
the books are gone now,
we rely on ourselves.

Dredge deeply, and find in the muck
with remorseless fingers
something solid.

Grasp it and hold
as if your fingers were frozen,
afraid of letting go.

Amazingly we pull it up
and wash it clean
and recognize it as nothing new.

ZEN AND KANT

Zen should be synonymous with spiritual narcissism.
Without faith, our thoughts are no more
important than a sparrow's.
Sure, our minds are equipped for logic;
but is logic any better than instinct... really?
Our minds are also equipped for faith.
To deny faith is to deny logic *and* instinct.
Have faith.
Then enjoy the gifts of logic and instinct,
which are hard-wired.
The only difference between the computer chip
and us is...?
And the prize goes to...!
Used to be us and the animals.
I think the animals have a leg up.
Screw Zen.

PEOPLE

It truly is amazing how a little stress evinces the subconscious thought processes. Ron once sent me a *Harper's* article about misanthropy. One of the lines went more or less like this: "We love the misanthrope because he is without prejudice. He hates everyone equally regardless of race, religion or political persuasion." Well, I haven't reached that level yet, but my cynicism has escalated to new heights. It really isn't "people" who cause problems but a very specific sort of people. You know the type: abrasive, arrogant without authority, unreasonable, uncompromising, etc. These folks leave as their signature a wake of frustration, animosity, and distrust even among those who throw a wake of peace, compassion, patience, and understanding. We must hold in our hearts that secure belief that when these waves meet, they will offset each other, resulting in the calm serenity that existed before they walked into our lives. And oh I could go on.

LIFE

Who can say where the limits of self-preservation lie?
In order to enjoy life one must want to live,
and in order to live one must enjoy life.
Where does the limit of our need for self-preservation lie?
At the boundary of our self-satisfaction?
Near the outermost regions of our ability to
comprehend our purpose?
Perhaps the important question is
how we rationalize our being as a worthwhile phenomenon.
There are just so many phenomenons.
We are all caught in the self-inflicted hierarchy of phenomenons.
Is there some inherent, purposeful end to this perpetual madness?
Why should I participate?
The causal link between self-preservation and the
ubiquitous madness of society
must be the instinctual philanthropy of mankind.
Many live simply to do good for others,
many live simply to do good for themselves.
Those who do good for others have the strongest desire and
enjoyment of life.
Those who do good for themselves proclaim a strong desire and
enjoyment of life,
but cannot possibly understand their purpose.

When we actually sit at the edge of our need for self-preservation,
we begin to see not only what is wrong and right but
more importantly how *we* have been wrong or right.
The sadness comes from the realization of this tardy discovery.
Had we been aware, had we been concerned with others,
we would have noticed in their faces the wrongness or rightness
of our actions.

It is this often neglected information that could prevent
our loss of esteem
and open our consciousness to our real purpose.
The need for self-preservation will then drift into our being,
never to be contemplated or aroused.

"I now re-write my limits of self-preservation poem from 1982"

What a shame that the best and the brightest have chosen
to be doctors. They've allowed their compassion to come between
them and self-fulfillment. Sacrifice is the name of the game.
Give the decade of youth and excitement in exchange
for education and the hope that your good efforts will
result in the physical enrichment of some poor, unlucky
soul's life. Thank God for doctors, the good ones, who
truly dedicate themselves to being the best. As for those
of us who utilize medicine as a means of making a good
wage, or becoming an important member of society, fuck
you. You have missed the point.

I have lost my only true colleague. He was a
physician and philosopher. I have lost the time available
to be those; as now, I have to be a good son, father,
husband, boss, leader, counselor, friend, and teacher.
My time is up. The ability to be at the leading edge
of my profession has slipped away. Thank God for
people like my erstwhile partner who have educated me about
true evil. He and very few others have helped me
cope with the reality of fatuousness. (Or is it fatuosity?)
I praise those who realize that they are only here for
a brief moment and it is important to make a point.
Just like in law school or med school when the student
has the ephemeral moment of satisfaction when he or
she impresses the teacher and achieves that grin
of appreciation, knowing that the student has
achieved intellectual nirvana.

Help Help Help. Not me; others. Watch out for the
ones who sidle, hoping to assimilate or
affect your character traits. As complimentary as it
may seem, tell them (nicely) to go away. Live your
life and teach. Live Live Live. And when you
die, don't worry. You've done the best you could.

A EULOGY

Succor to the merchants of fear
he carries on the doomsday tradition,
too much carbon dioxide, global warming!

So what?
The "plants" will live, I said.
Each day the world becomes a little worse.

Just because he had no row to hoe
doesn't mean I can't have the whole field.
Take the whole field, he'd say
it might teach you limitations.

Then he would place the sugar in the gas tank of my tractor.

So what?
The plants "will" live, I said,
but each day the world becomes a little worse.

Bless this food to the nourishment of our bodies,
he prays to his god,
until his body will take nourishment no more.
We place his body at last into the earth.

So what?
The plants will "live," I say.
But this day the world has become a little worse.

THE EDGE

Consider boundaries.
A meadow meets the forest,
the twilight meets the darkness,
the lake meets the shore,
the air meets the surface of a stream
with its swirling ebbs and eddies
belying the structures beneath.
What else can greater spark
imagination and desire than these boundary zones,
which contrast vastly different arrays of sensation.
Boundaries provide us with variety fused into one whole
and made vivid by the mind's desire to know two things
at once.

•   •   •   •   •

JOHN'S SONG

Fat fucking middle-aged man
starved for youth
feeding on loss
or what could have been.
Don't suck from me
just suck me.
You flailing bag of desperate catshit,
wanna be,
could have been,
but you ain't.
Tried to fill your sails with wind
but your sheets were soiled.
Stuck together
like your two remaining brain cells
in need of company.

MY VALLEY

I have cast a fly onto the River of Life,
which lies between two eternities
and come up empty.

As the river flows between ranges,
I try to get a glimpse
over the mountains.

Vain attempts to see what lies
on the other side are met with
a rush of current.

Swept off my feet,
floating freely, I begin to realize
it doesn't matter.

Trust that the current may carry me
safely down the stream
I yield to its power.

That same force that formed my valley
touches and calms me
and looks kindly on my drift.

It allows me to slip quietly,
peacefully, into the delta
at the end of the River valley.

FISHING FOOLS

I turn my head and start to yawn
when you speak of using spawn,
because, you see, to serve this dish
one must assume you've killed a fish.

These eggs were meant to reproduce,
it doesn't take Einstein to deduce
that trout must do this to survive
why don't you let them go alive.

And as for hardware, lead, and spoons
all these could spell the fish's doom.
They litter logs and rocks and trees
these models of efficiency.

These things aren't in a fish's diet,
why don't you add some salt and try it.
You line the banks and drink your beer
and leave your garbage there and here,

and keep your fish hung on your stringers,
you lure- and worm- and spawn-bag flingers.
There's no respect among your lot
for the fish that you have caught.

A grand and beautiful creature once
goes to the stomach of a dunce.
Seafood's cheaper at the store
and if you want thrills go get a whore,

and keep your fat ass off my stream.
But, of course, I know that's just a dream.

FOUR YEARS LATER

Well, I'm four years
into it.
Or is it three?

You see,
part of me went away
that day.

And one year later
most of me went away,
as I said goodbye.

We choked back tears,
my friend and I,
the first time.

The second time struck
artesian wells of tears
which flow only at night.

When no one can see
my pain,
which everyone can see in their own light.

THE FRONT PORCH

Ask your neighbor,
he may know not only the answer,
but the reason you are asking.
He may care.
We have lost the front porch
from which to wave at our neighbors,
to show we care.
We have lost the country kitchen
where family sits with friends at the end of the day
offering support.
Individualism has become misguided,
nocturnal, eschewing the light of fellowship.
Because others have helped us
makes us no less unique.
Ah, the communal life could expose our weaknesses,
but don't we all have our foibles?
We can learn from others if we want to,
and thus educated
we, if brilliant or creative to start with,
can leave a much more meaningful legacy.
Someday, perhaps
someone may learn something from us.

TO A SAD FRIEND

Smile with me little brother
and don't let the world coat you
with a carapace of gloom and despair.
Give me a signal of your sadness
and I will be there,
smiling and laughing to cheer you.
We must live and not just prepare to die.
Life is not a preparation for death
but a gift that we must enjoy before it spoils,
like a good steak.
There are many wrongs and evils,
not all your responsibility,
please don't bear that burden
but live your life by example so that others
may see the inherent benefits of so clean and pure an existence.
Anger, greed, and jealousy
will tear at the heart of your soul;
but defend against these as strongly as a threat to life itself
for indeed these are a threat to real life and living.
The good will find the good.
Be patient and these and theirs will present themselves in good time,
but guard against the false ones because they will destroy you.

THE TRUTH

Significant songs
wound through the harp strings of our soul,
unplucked, unpluckable,
tangential to life
they lie
sorrowful and silent
awaiting age to reveal their timeless import.
Watching as crowds pass by oblivious.
A future miner strikes gold,
a rich vein, strewn carelessly upon a written page
never publicized.
It hearkens to the depths of our being,
gives strength.
Anguish, that the words once spoken fell upon stone,
when fertile soil lay nearby.
A blink could be decades, centuries,
yet, as the great one planned
it is only a microsecond.
In the end the truth is all revealed.
Until then, we have free will to get us through the days,
knowing the beauty,
the glory of that music, which man has created and will
continue to be discovered
and understood.

ODE TO THE SPECIMEN JAR

Oh I wish I were a specimen jar
so I could hold specimens from near and afar

the snot from the nose, the mucous from the throat,
the urine and feces and things that don't float,

like gallstones and tumors and pimples of course,
and moles and rashes and lymph nodes and warts.

And the worst thing of all, for which there isn't a term,
a tiny receptacle to hold all my sperm.

The thing is so tiny, the mouth is so small,
it's a wonder I could hit that damn thing at all.

But when it's all over, when everythings done,
I'll just deny everything, and say it was fun.

A CHRISTMAS FIGHT

'Twas the week before Christmas
and all through the house
there was dirt everywhere,
she was mad at her spouse.

The dishes were nestled all over the sink,
the ice box was empty, there was nothing to drink.
When what through the clouds of dust should appear,
but a double cheese pizza and a six pack of beer.

He farted and slurped and made such a clatter
She yelled from the couch, "You'll only get fatter!"
"I'm getting more beer," he said as he squeezed through the door,
then he slipped on the dog shit that lay on the floor.

He sat there for a moment and looked down at his belly,
and thought to himself, her feet sure are smelly.
"Come here honey, I think that I'm sick,"
but he knew then and there it must be a trick.

So on hands and on knees he crawled through the kitchen,
through the dog hair, the mold, and the scum without bitchin'
then on to the bedroom where she lay there in waiting,
all naked and lusty and ready for mating.

She grabbed onto his penis and as it went out of sight,
He said, "I love you honey, let's make this our last fight."

INTRO TO AN ESSAY

Had an idea for *Esquire*: "Dances with Women" (a real man's guide through relationships). Alt. title: "Men Are From Mars, Women Are From Venus is Crap."

At some point in every man's life, a woman will break his heart. Having been through the tinker toy repair of my own myriad times, I now wish to bequeath to my brethren (sparing alliteration) boatfuls of beleaguered ballast, which may raise you back to the surface of things and prevent you from diving deep into thought about things you are not capable of understanding. I have no degree in psychology, but I am a surgeon and have studied most of philosophy and religion as taught at higher levels. More importantly, I was raised in a family that held traditional moral values as paramount to any auspicious credentials or notoriety.

Women are devious. They devour, delight, design, discuss (ad nauseum), deprecate us, diminish us, develop themselves, defend their inferiority, demand equality, define our roles, dignify Mary Magdalene, and dig our graves emotionally from the inception of a relationship with the genuine hope of being the first to toss a fistful of dirt onto the casket. After lying in my own casket for several years, I finally decided that the worms could wait and threw the daisies aside. Read on and you will learn that not only are women okay, but that they have something to teach us, which I heretofore have not seen on the roster of college courses offered in this solar system.

Have you ever looked into a woman's eyes during casual conversation and seen something that convinced you that "she" was special. That "she" was the one for you and at the very least you could run back to some convenient billet and accommodate your desire forthwith? You will discover that there are few reasons why this innate behavior, which has been written about for centuries, romanticized, studied, rhapsodized, and sullied, is entirely out of our control.

I hope to, in this plebian monologue, give men a real reason to be skeptical about relationships with women as we think we understand them. After all, once we understand something, we can deal with it... right?

RANDOM THOUGHTS

Stupidity is ultimately forgivable,
but ignorance should be punished
as a felony.

Contrary to popular belief, the
average life is difficult to fill.

Unfortunately, women know that
men are assholes.

I wish I knew what was really
going on in one square inch of my
backyard.

Define infinity in terms I can comprehend
and then reiterate how you don't believe
in God.

Zeno only got halfway there.

99% of people believe that 1% of all
people control the world. 1% of people
have accepted the fact that 99% of people
control the world.

Did God create love, or did love
create God?

Everything in moderation,
including moderation.

HEX-A-GONE

Short summer,
but good things can come in short packages.
Fishing the *Hexagenias* under a full moon on a dead calm evening
with coyotes yipping in the background.
Grouse drumming ten feet away on the river bank.
Fireflies signaling their presence as deliquescent dusk heralds the
onset of the spinner fall.
Winged angels of the insect world, exciting me more than the trout
and carrying me to one of life's most heavenly experiences.
Close to nature, close to God (if she exists),
and as close as one can come to sex while vertical.
A two-foot trout, piscatorial masterpiece,
spots gleaming under flashlight held in teeth,
mouth agape like mine,
slides to hand while barbless hook is slipped from its berth and
after meticulous revival eases embarrassed to the river bottom
attempting to regain orientation.
Trembling hands fumbling to remove the annihilated fly
and find new fare in the metal box,
leader trimmed back to six feet and ten pound
because the fish no longer care.
Trout, large trout
continue to feed less than five feet away,
coaxing me to hurry with my task but the new fly drops to the current
and is swept away for a second, until
slurp.
Hopefully he didn't take it down too far.
The pace slows and I'm finally prepared to resume the chase
but something has changed.
All is quiet.

Only the whip-poor-will stirs the air with his
plaintive cry and subtle buzz.
What was full of life has given way to paranoid stillness.
It can't be over, it can't.
Half the time had been spent struggling in darkness,
focused on a task as simple as tying on a fly.
Grace under pressure.
I once knew a girl named Grace, I never had her.
The walk back to the truck follows, the trail displayed to my
retinal rods by the moonlight,
the sweet smell of the night air, the whine of my bird dog
from the truck as he detects my approach,
the friend arriving shortly thereafter uncorking a bottle of wine,
the toast, the calm sigh,
the sharing of evening events unembellished,
the tired drive home, the kiss from my wife, the dreams,
and the next day the sun rising... again.

SPORTSPALS

No, this is not an essay on lightweight aluminum canoes, or friends involved in athletics. I wish instead to explore the factors that make us all the ideal partner in outdoor sporting pursuits. Let us first break down the relationship that you have with your sporting companions into several useful and meaningful categories:

1) *Timeliness.* A rendezvous with you is like money in the bank for your partners. We are all very busy, and it seems that time spent afield with rod or gun is harder to come by with each passing year. Your partners have always been able to count on your punctuality. You would sooner stick needles in your eyes than cause your pal to miss the hatch by being late. In fact, you're usually early, always offering to help with any last-minute preparations to ensure a successful and pleasurable excursion. Yes sir, even though your partner left you at the bar last night so you could "finish that last drink" or "break the ice with the attractive blonde," he knew in the depths of his soul that you would be there on time the next morning with a thermos of coffee and donuts for everyone.

2) *Common sense.* Anyone who has spent enough time in the woods or on the water understands that there will be occasional, well, unfortunate mishaps. It is during these times of stress that you always come through, offering solutions based on your sound fundamental knowledge of woodsmanship, easing tensions that can so easily arise during times of great anxiety. You even add a tinge of humor to lighten a seemingly hopeless situation. So many sportsmen are afflicted with partners who have at best a room temperature I.Q. If they are lost together, they stay lost. If they are having an unsuccessful day afield, the next day will most likely be unsuccessful as well. You, on the other hand, not only know how to prevent bad things from happening, but if per chance they do, you always know how to make the best of a bad situation.

3) *Humility.* Nothing is quite so odious as a braggart. As Jim Harrison so eloquently stated, "... any spirit of competition in hunting or fishing dishonors the prey." Even though you consistently catch more fish than your partners, largely due to pure natural ability, you never gloat or depreciate your partners' abilities but humbly minimize the importance of numbers relative to an aesthetic appreciation of the sport. You casually offer suggestions based on a technique you "accidentally stumbled upon" that might help your pal improve his catch. You are patient with the beginner, understanding that "we all make mistakes, that's why they put rubber on the end of pencils."

4) *Talkability.* Henry VanDyke, one of the most deft wordsmen of the late nineteenth century, explored this topic in detail. Talkability is not the same as talkativeness, which can be inexorably boring and one-sided. Talkability is also unlike eloquence in that an eloquent person is impressive to listen to but largely intolerant of interruption. Oratory in general is self-centered and uncommunicative. As VanDyke states, "A talkable person, therefore, is one whose nature and disposition invite the easy interchange of thoughts and feelings, one in whose company it is a pleasure to talk or to be talked to." Nuf said.

5) *Graciousness.* You are kind and courteous to a fault. My father (and probably many others) used to carry a spent shotgun shell in his bird-hunting vest. When grouse would flush and his pal made a good shot, he would slip the empty into the chamber and walk up asking with a surprised expression, "Did you shoot, too?" The joke would be revealed in short order but that brief moment of doubt on the part of his partner used to just tickle him pink. When it came to a true simultaneous shot that dropped the bird, he was always first to relinquish the prize, even though he was relatively sure his partner had missed the mark by a considerable margin (judging from the shot pattern on the mature birch tree). Similarly, you encourage your partner to fish your favorite hole because you want him to experience the same enjoyment you have known there. Then, you move on

downstream to lesser water but not too far away to witness your friend having the time of his life. This truly makes you happy.

6) *Generosity.* Many partners are quite consistent in their ability to forget certain essential items when embarking on an outdoor excursion. Thank goodness they have you along. Your forethought to throw in that extra spool of tippet material or tie an extra dozen flies has saved the day for your pals many times. You always offer to pay for gasoline in exchange for the privileges of riding instead of driving. You always offer to bring food enough for everyone on the trip, you cook (well) and even do the dishes at camp. You are usually the one to pick up the tab at the bar after it has circulated around the table like a hot potato, and come holiday time you remember your pals with that poignant gift, that special piece of equipment they mentioned a need for several months earlier.

7) *Expertise.* Knowledge is power. Your research, both didactic and practical, has positioned you to be the envy of all your sporting companions. Sure you know the Latin but rarely use it at the risk of seeming aloof. Nevertheless, when it comes to ending an argument over whether the last duck was a hen ringneck or a hen redhead, you are the consummate ornithologist. Your familiarity with local waters and the trout that inhabit them makes fishing with you better than a day with the best and most expensive guide in the area. You know the names of all the local trees and shrubs and have most recently developed an interest in wildflowers. You can converse intelligently about anything from classic literature to best guns, classical music to rap, Beaujolais to Boone's Farm.

Being one to almost always be late, get lost in a paper bag, argue about who actually caught the biggest trout, interrupt during conversations, never divulge my favorite fishing spots, claim that I have no cash when the tab comes, and couldn't tell a mallard from a ruddy duck, I am always in search of the ideal outdoor companion. So the next time you need to fill a seat in your boat, I promise I will come along quietly, willing to listen and learn.

NUF'S NUF

As I drove home from work tonight, winter in Northern Michigan, the pastel pinks, oranges, reds, and finally much closer to the horizon, the blues (just as in music) contrasted nicely against the purity, the whiteness of the snow blowing across the road, creating hazardous footing for my vehicle. I began to think about the beauty and the purity of the fly-fishing endeavor relative to well-adorned and seemingly gracious attempts by authors down through history, which have recreated the glorious experiences and knowledge they have accrued and provided us with "informational literature."

One fact has held true for me for the last thirty years. The best fishermen I know are not widely quoted. Their autographs exist only at the bottom of checks they use at the end of each month to pay their bills, yet they are as knowledgeable as any text I have read myself, and are able to temper their knowledge with a humbleness that can only be derived by consistently being outwitted by trout.

I do not intend to demean the fly-fishing literary elite. Their altruism to the sport and contributions to the technical advancement of fishing efficiency have allowed many of those who would otherwise never find the time, to discover the seemingly obvious mechanisms of coaxing a trout to take a fly, playing the fish, landing it, and releasing it, to effectively displace the uneducated from many a run, riffle, or pool. Unfortunately, their introductions to new, exotic, isolated, and expensive locations have lured (so to speak) many anglers both worthy and unworthy, to these locations, thus diminishing the specialness of the region. One might suggest that the more presumptuous writers develop a usufructuary arrangement with the sport rather than exploiting its popularity for the sake of personal gain or ego. Fly-fishing literature is replete with saprophytic individual works that obviously hope to provide the author with a technical "fish ladder," enabling them to climb to heights recognized as expert.

Fly-fishing as sport is sacred. It is, and will always be, manifest in exultation of the individual mastering his or her quarry. Tell me a fish story, but please stop telling me how or where to fish. I'd rather figure that out for myself, thank you. The burgeoning boundaries of fly-fishing literature have created an overpopulation of our streams these days because it is popular, cool, delicate, or even intellectual. Whatever banal adjective we choose, fly-fishing will always be an individual sport, enjoyed the most by those who dedicate their time to its intricacies actively—not by sitting on the couch reading about it. If only Dame Juliana would have kept her mouth shut.

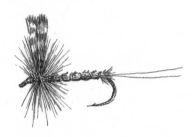

FOR STARTERS

Remember watching old T.V. commercials and seeing the guy with his spinning reel held on top of the rod handle, reeling backwards with the wrong hand? You'd smugly chuckle at the ignorance of the producer. How could anyone not know how to hold a spinning rod? It's awfully easy, as well, to critique the beginning fly caster whose 3 to 9 range of motion yields the telltale wide loops and slaps on the water fore and aft, with that final energetic forward cast intended to straighten out the whole mess and propel the imaginary Rapala toward its target. Old habits die hard. Watching a youngster with his first Donald Duck Zebco reel try to perfect his timing at the thumb release can be amusing at first, eventually frustrating for his or her teacher, and ultimately exhilarating as the worm and bobber sail that perfect arc... into the trees across the pond.

Trees. How many of us spent the first several years learning how to fly cast and climb trees at the same time, trying to retrieve loops and snarls of line, leader, and tippet just out of reach and ultimately ripping our waders to shreds (usually with applause from those passing by in canoes)? I can't tell you how many times a canoeist has caught me on tiptoes reaching for my fly in a tree limb and said, "You'd probably catch more fish in the water." No comment.

There's also an art to wading. Early on I was provided by my father with a pair of hip waders, which I know were designed to keep me just far enough away from a rising trout to tempt disaster. It always seemed I needed just a couple more inches. Once again I'm on tiptoes. The various styles and forms of falling into the river could be the subject of an elaborate photo essay, the problem is that the spontaneity of the event precludes reasonable camera work. I have performed such incredible athletic maneuvers trying to remain vertical in a stream that my wife's ballet teacher would probably be envious. The end result is always the same; no matter how hard I try to be cool after one of these "seizures," I remain embarrassed, praying that no one saw me. When I am fortunate enough to witness a friend stumble, pirouette, spin, flail, and eventually take the plunge, the laughter spills forth like water from a broken dam. It is sheer, unadulterated hilarity, usually met by a scowl and a curse from the victim.

Over the years, I've learned to step carefully and have been educated about the "buddy system," where two anglers walk abreast with an arm around each other's shoulders. If you've never tried this in difficult water, you should. It can save a good soaking, sprained ankles, and a lot of lost gear.

I'll never forget the first time I heard the word *Ephemerella*. My junior high buddy pompously blurted it out one day while we were talking about an upcoming fly fishing excursion on the AuSable. "Yeah, the *Ephemerellas* will be popping today for sure," he said. I was too proud to ask him what the hell he was talking about as I assumed that a bug was a bug and that the Adam's hatch was all I cared about anyway. I always caught fish when they were hatching, and I even knew how to tie one. The next year, I read Selective Trout, by Swisher and Richards, and subtly worked my way into the dialect of the fly fisherman. Since then, that book has become dog-eared and worn and the Adam's hatch has taken on an obvious and less important meaning.

Learning how to fish can be simultaneously the most enjoyable and frustrating of all life's experiences. The key is in finding a patient and knowledgeable teacher and spending many hours alone, working things out for ourselves to avoid the litany of harsh critiques that are often freely handed out by our fellow anglers. We should all be encouraging to our lesser-experienced comrades, and when they do fall into the river... try not to laugh.

HOW TO PLAN A TRIP

I had decided to take a weekend for myself, reading and writing about the things I held closest in my chest. Fly-fishing and bird hunting were the avocations I had cut my teeth on, but recent turns-of-events necessitated a re-prioritization of time allotted for these special pursuits in favor of family life and hard work. Early morning and late evening meetings, weekends dedicated to shopping and chores around the house, were starting to take their toll.

The pleasure of a wonderful woman, and the fatherly pride inherent in watching my beautiful boy and girl take their first steps and begin to speak intelligibly made my bubble of happiness nearly burst; but the presence of my quartet of flyrods sitting idly in the corner of the den and the fey, half-hearted glances from my bird dog gradually began plucking at the harpstrings of my soul so harmoniously that I knew a change was about to take place.

A good friend and guide in Montana had phoned after I made a recent trip there with my wife. "Ken, you absolutely have to come back in the fall for a cast and blast. We have more pheasant, sharptails, ducks, and geese than I've ever seen before, and when we're limited out by noon we get to fish the rest of the day."

"Okay Donny," I said, "I'll think about it, but life is definitely different now. I'll call you and let you know."

As I read that weekend, my thoughts turned more inward than outward. How was I to be a good husband and father without "following the bent of my genius" as Thoreau said? The fall trip planning commenced. As I sat with a copy of *Gray's Sporting Journal* in my lap, my wife was muttering something about not getting out of the house for two years.

Should I take the old Parker or the Beretta? Since I'd be flying, should I take my beloved Brittany or settle for Donny's

Labradors? "I'm serious," she said, "all I do is stay home, watch our children, and do your laundry."

Who would be my companion on the trip? Would it be my local hunting/fishing partner, or my long-time friend and good sport from Chicago?

"Are you ever going to finish that project in the pole-barn, or am I going to have to do it myself... are you listening to me?"

More birds than ever? Limited out by noon? Flip streamers and look for heads until dark? Sip Manhattans with a good friend at the end of the day and dine on a great Montana steak dinner? Share and compare fishing vignettes with other sports from around the world?

"I'm serious, if you don't watch these children and give me some alone time, I'm out of here."

I have to call my travel agent tomorrow and check on the airfares. No wait, I can use frequent-flyer miles and save the money for the trip to Belize with my wife this winter. She'll like that.

"Dammit, I'm to the breaking point, I need a man that cares about me... do you hear me?"

The door slammed as she left. No doubt to spend the night with her mom and dad who had just discovered their middle-aged, retirement-phase interest called Harley-Davidson riding. Since I can't stand anything loud except the report of a shotgun or a thunderstorm, I am, needless to say, less than supportive of their endeavors.

I finished my last article, called my friend in Chicago, and poured a glass of good bourbon. I was playing with my bird dog on the floor when she returned two hours later.

"The babes are bathed, changed, fed, and in bed," I proudly reported. "Oh, and by the way, I've decided to go to Montana with Ron this fall."

PEACEFUL DAYS ASTREAM

I am never more free than when approaching trout with a flyrod. That total absolution from the workaday world comes at the expense of a brow-wrenching intensity of concentration that purifies one, purging the mundane pressures of the occupation, the domestic duties, and social obligations found away from the stream. I've often felt ill-at-ease with the dichotomy between my profession of medicine and the simple purity of plotting to take a trout on the dry fly. Necessity dictates that I must approach both with an honest intensity, but the fact of the matter is that medicine is largely empirical and fly-fishing is, or should be, mostly right-brain. An almost schizophrenic paranoia sometimes descends on me as I depart on a destination fishing trip, eager to escape those who fatuously plod through life not realizing that their weekly trips to the therapist could be entirely substituted by a few peaceful days astream. I wish to, as Thoreau stated, follow the creative bent of my genius, and let it carry me daily to water that holds trout.

Having held a flyrod literally since I was a toddler further emphasizes the disparity between profession and my preferred leisure-time pursuits. Fly-fishing is solitary. The single-minded focus on the quarry inherently obliterates in seconds all information that stabs at my consciousness constantly when at work. Sure, there is a genuine caring and concern for the people, my patients, but the burden of their dependence is shed as I plop a bit of tobacco in the cul-de-sac of my lower lip, strip line off the reel, and begin the false-casting approach to the slurping aquatic destination for my number 18 blue-winged olive. The mind absorbs all the relative factors to complete the ruse. After a time, we develop a gestalt of the situation, simultaneously factoring wind direction, river speed, light conditions, and method of approach necessary to complete the task at hand. The ultimate determinant of our success (defined as tricking the trout into believing that your fly represents an opportunity for sustenance) is the ability to assimilate all the information at hand and regurgitate it in one magnificent creative blow. When it all comes together there is an ethereal, anticipatory jubilation that is, as they say, better than sex.

That's when it all comes together. Chances are good that our attempts at creativity will rival those of a fourth grade writing assignment rather than a Shakespearean masterpiece. We are thusly... humbled.

Fly-fishers have, in general, a justifiable condescension to the rest of the world. Who, after all, repeatedly experiences the most beautiful places on earth, witnesses the drama of nature close at hand, and holds all of this close to our hearts with a reverence rivaling Christmas mass at St. Peter's Cathedral? Thoughts of trout and the environs in which they are found lurk constantly in our subconscious minds, even when at work or clinking a toast at a cocktail party. I firmly believe there is a genetic predisposition to becoming a fly-fisherman and that this trait runs parallel to our generally calm and courtly demeanor. If only everyone could share this mental state, the world would be a better place. On the other hand, I'm glad everyone doesn't.

THE MASON TRACT
(As originally published in *Journeys North*, Autumn 2002)

Yesterday, my wife Marilyn and I slid our canoe into the quiet water below Chase Bridge and loaded our cargo of two toddlers and one Brittany into the middle, replete with life vests and shock collars. The immediate serenity influenced our actions as we stocked the canoe with a half day's supply of food and drink, scarcely noticing the occasional passing car. The river was a bit turbid from early spring rains and the banks were flooded beyond what I was used to after many years of fishing during mid-summer nights for large brown trout. Nevertheless, the river was in very good shape for a wonderful half day drift.

"Buckle that vest up buddy," I told Zane as we drifted away from the launch. We had spotted a car about fourteen river miles downstream at Smith Bridge which is just off M-72. This would be our takeout point, which we knew we could reach in about seven hours, with a little effort. The problem was that there was so much to see along the way... or was it so little? The stretch we were canoeing has always been held in my heart as the holiest of holy water. Thirteen miles of river and thousands of acres of the surrounding land was bequeathed to the State of Michigan by Mr. George Mason in 1954. In exchange, Mr. Mason requested that the area be left undeveloped and that all existing structures be left alone to eventually return the area to its natural state.

Mr. Mason was the president of the Nash-Kelvinator Corporation which evolved into American Motors. He was the quintessential conservationist and his dictum was that fishing with other than a flyrod put the river in a "meat market" class. Since his death, the river eventually achieved "flies only" status, and much of the Mason Tract is now catch-and-release fishing only. His reverence for the river gradually developed into a wonderful coterie of environmentalists, most notably, George Griffith, who founded Trout Unlimited.

As we drifted around the first few bends and settled into our afternoon reverie, my children suddenly quieted for the first time in weeks. "Daddy, what was that big bird?" they asked. I explained that the kingfisher guarded the river, and that the sound it made was more of a cry of exultation than a warning. The female wood ducks whistled their spring call as they flew up the river runway, and a flock of geese announced their presence with a flurry of honks and whistles. The lilies and watercress proclaimed that spring had finally arrived and random lilacs scattered their wonderful fragrance over the beautiful unique and pristine water. My son leaned over the bow of the canoe and saw several large trout suspended in a deeper run. Turning to me with raised brow he said, "Daddy, I saw a very big trout right under our canoe."

"Yes Zane, I know. Look up ahead, do you see the family of mink over there?" The little fur balls suddenly began swimming across the river and a few of the stragglers ended up bumping into the side of our canoe, confused for a moment, and then continued, trying to follow their mother to the other side of the stream. Our children were speechless.

Eventually, about a mile further, my son asked, "Daddy, did those mink babies ever find their mommy?" After a brief moment of introspection, I decided to tell him that their mommy came back and pulled every single one of them to the shore. After all, mommies do that.

We stopped for lunch at the Castle, one of the two designated rest points for canoes on the river. This area has outhouse facilities, trash receptacles, and a wonderful bulletin board with photos and a history of "Durant's Castle," a fifty-two room mansion constructed around 1920 at that site. Only remnants of the structure's foundation are still visible today. Mr. Durant was the founder of General Motors, and more importantly, a lover of this wonderful river. A tremendous sense of awe overtook me as I read the history of the area and looked at the early photographs. It was wonderful to share a reverence for this country eighty years after Mr. Durant had shared similar sentiments with his own family. A porcupine sat calmly in a large pine watching my reminiscence. I'm sure he awaited dusk to descend upon the plywood structure in search of sustenance.

After lunch, we floated along past the High Banks, the Baldwin's, and stopped briefly at the second designated area, the Fisherman's Chapel. Constructed on a particularly scenic bend in the river, there is a long dock along the outside bank. As we looked up the steep hillside covered with towering White Pines, we saw the small stone structure with slate roof. Mr. Mason ordered this to be built in the fifties, but he passed away prior to its completion. It was to be the only maintained site on the entire thirteen mile stretch of river, a place where fisherman and canoeists could stop, seek shelter, enjoy the pristine environment, and take time to contemplate God's wonderful creation. "Daddy, is this a church?" my daughter Zoe asked.

"Sort of sweetheart, it's definitely a place to stop and count our blessings." We solemnly proceeded downstream to Downey's where you can see the remnants of the old fieldstone wall and steps of the Downey House, which was a fishing destination back in the twenties. Mr. Downey was also one of the original owners of this property, prior to Mr. Durant. We stopped briefly to examine the stone structures and admire the ancient willow now guarding the site.

We floated on peacefully to Smith Bridge, enjoying our uninterrupted family time and talking about all we had seen: the variety of the river with bends, virgin pine woods next to well managed "cuts," unadulterated tributaries with beaver, otter, muskrat, mink, weasel, rabbits, grouse, turkey, woodcock, ducks, geese, frogs, dragonflies, damselflies, all varieties of mayfly, caddis, stone flies, butterflies, bluebirds, one Kirtland's warbler (we think), swallows, nighthawks, and as we pulled out at Smith Bridge, bats. The children were not quite sure about them. On the ride home, my wife and I commented on what a perfectly serene day it had been. We both felt so relaxed and at ease with ourselves and the world. I couldn't help feeling sorry for those who cannot find the time to take a gentle float down this river. It genuinely is cathartic. Keep that in mind and consider trying it, and remember George Mason and his reverence for this wonderful gift to us all.

IN MEMORY OF DR. THOMAS C. HALL
(As originally published in *The Pointing Dog Journal*,
July/August 2004)

He came to the stream, and paused for a moment at the bridge. He wanted to tell them he was happy, if only they knew how happy he was, but when he opened his eyes he could not see them anymore. Everything else was bright, but the room was dark.

The bell had stopped, and he looked across the stream. The other side was bathed in sunshine, and he could see the road mounting steeply, and the clearing in the woods, and the apple tree in a corner of the stone wall. Shad was standing, motionless, beneath it, the white fan of his tail lifted, his neck craned forward and one foreleg cocked. The whites of his eyes showed as he looked back, waiting for him.

"Steady," he called, "Steady, boy." He started across the bridge. "I'm coming."

George Bird Evans said that "the greatest trouble with bird dogs is that you have them with you for so short a while." As I recollected this comment after the death of my dear friend and hunting partner, Doc Hall, it occurred to me that we have too short a time to spend with our human sporting companions as well. Tom passed away peacefully in his sleep on the morning of February 25th, 2004, at the too young age of 68. His malady was liver failure due to hepatitis C contracted while performing surgery over a decade ago. He called his terminal illness "clumsy surgeon's disease."

Think of the person you respect the most in your life right now. Throw in an Ivy League education, extensive knowledge of bird dogs and upland birds, a keen wit, absolute humility, genuine concern, generosity, professionalism, and a long list of athletic accomplishments, and that would be Tom. He was the living, breathing paradigm of the ideal hunting companion and friend.

Even at 68, Tom was amazingly fit. He played rugby regularly until just a few years ago and started a local rugby club in his hometown; the clubhouse is on the banks of a fine trout stream just south of town (not by coincidence).

If you didn't know Tom, you probably know of his older brother Jim, also a physician, and the model for Corey Ford's "Doc Hall" in the *Stories of the Lower Forty*. Jim is retired now and has established himself as a fine outdoor essayist with several books and many articles to his credit. Tom and Jim both lived with Corey in a flat outside the boundaries of Dartmouth College in New Hampshire while attending school there.

Their father, Dr. James Hall, and Bill Wicksall were involved in the first woodcock banding efforts in the United States. They also developed their own line of English setters, which Tom, along with Bill Wicksall's daughter Sally and her husband Dave Downer, have carried on.

At Tom's memorial service in Traverse City, Michigan, more than 500 people gathered to pay their respects. He asked that Corey Ford's *Road to Tinkhamtown* be read to his friends, the last couple paragraphs of which appear above and are an apt tribute to all departed hunting companions out there.

Tom's passing has left a monstrous void in my life. He was mentor, friend, intellectual rival, comic, and a true inspiration. He will be missed in many areas around the world for his conservation efforts. As another friend of Tom's noted, "He was just one of those people who lived life brilliantly."

I am humbled that Tom has bequeathed his two-year-old setter pup, Jody, to me. He allowed me to participate in her early training when he was away in New Zealand, and she will be welcomed as a member of our family. Some of his last words before passing were, "She's a smart dog, and I know you'll take good care of her." I cannot think of any greater honor. He mentioned on several occasions that we were "kindred spirits," and I believe there are many of us out there.

The next time you load up your dogs and pile into the truck with your hunting buddy, take a moment to silently appreciate what you have sitting next to you. Because there is a reason that person is sitting there, and at least in my case, it ended way too soon.